Financial Mast[ery]
From [...]

DI TRAN [UNIVERSITY]
LOUISVILLE BEAUTY ACADEMY

FINANCIAL MASTERY FOR BEAUTY PROFESSIONALS
FROM $0 TO SALON EMPIRE

DI TRAN

Financial Mastery for Beauty Professionals:
From $0 to Salon Empire

Why You Should Read This Book

The beauty industry is a world of passion, creativity, and transformation. Every day, you, as a beauty professional, change lives—boosting confidence, inspiring self-love, and helping people feel their best. But while you're busy transforming others, are you also transforming your financial future?

This book isn't just another guide about making money; it's a roadmap to taking control of your life through financial mastery. It's for those who have the courage to dream big but want practical, step-by-step strategies to turn those dreams into reality. Whether you're a student at a beauty college, a newly licensed professional, or an experienced salon owner, this book will revolutionize how you think about money, investment, and growth.

Here are the reasons why this book is not just worth reading—it's essential for your success.

---

1. Money Isn't the Problem—It's How You Think About It

Money itself isn't the key to success; how you manage and use it is. Too often, beauty

Financial Mastery for Beauty Professionals:
From $0 to Salon Empire

professionals fall into the trap of emotional spending. It's easy to justify buying the latest tools, fancy decorations for your salon, or even indulging in personal luxuries to "treat yourself." But every dollar you spend emotionally is a dollar not working for your future.

This book will help you break free from emotional spending habits. You'll learn how to recognize the emotional triggers behind your spending, reframe your mindset, and redirect that money into opportunities that create real, lasting wealth. Imagine putting every dollar to work for you—not just to feel good today, but to secure your future for years to come.

---

2. Start Small, Dream Big: How to Grow from $0 to Salon Empire

No matter where you are in your career, you can start building wealth right now. Maybe you're working at someone else's salon, just beginning to learn the ropes. Maybe you're renting a booth and dreaming of owning your first salon. Or perhaps you already own a business but want to expand or create a chain of salons.

Financial Mastery for Beauty Professionals:
From $0 to Salon Empire

This book gives you the blueprint to grow step by step:

- **From working for someone else to becoming your own boss.**
- **From owning a small salon to building a salon empire.**
- **From earning a paycheck to creating passive income streams.**

Through practical strategies and real-life examples, this book will show you how to double your money, then double it again—and again. Success isn't about taking giant leaps; it's about small, consistent actions that compound over time.

---

3. Learn the Art of Smart Investments

The beauty industry can be incredibly rewarding, but it also has its challenges. Many beauty professionals don't think beyond their daily earnings, forgetting that smart investments can create wealth that works for them—even while they're asleep.

This book will teach you where to put your money so it grows:

Financial Mastery for Beauty Professionals:
From $0 to Salon Empire

- **Investing in yourself:** Education, skills, and certifications.
- **Investing in your business:** Tools, marketing, and team-building.
- **Investing in assets:** Real estate for your salon, stocks, and more.

You'll learn how to transition from renting a booth to owning the building where your salon operates. Why pay rent when you can pay yourself? Over time, this single shift can transform your finances, allowing you to build wealth through equity and appreciation.

---

4. Master Taxes and Legal Structures Like a Pro

One of the biggest mistakes beauty professionals make is not understanding how to manage their taxes and business expenses. By not structuring your business properly, you're likely paying more taxes than you need to and losing money that could be reinvested in your growth.

This book demystifies the tax system for beauty professionals:

- How to track and deduct expenses like supplies, tools, and education.

Financial Mastery for Beauty Professionals:
From $0 to Salon Empire

- Setting up your business legally to protect your assets and save on taxes.
- Turning personal expenses into legitimate business expenses.

You'll learn how to stop letting taxes eat into your hard-earned money and instead use them to your advantage.

---

5. Overcome the Emotional Barriers to Wealth

The beauty industry is full of talented individuals who never achieve financial success—not because they lack skill, but because they lack the right mindset. Fear, self-doubt, and limiting beliefs keep many professionals stuck in the same place, year after year.

This book is designed to help you overcome those barriers. Through actionable exercises and stories of others who've succeeded, you'll develop the confidence to:

- Take risks without fear of failure.
- Say no to short-term rewards for long-term gains.

Financial Mastery for Beauty Professionals:
From $0 to Salon Empire

- Build habits that lead to financial independence.

You'll also learn how to adopt a "wealth mindset," where you stop seeing money as something to spend and start seeing it as a tool to grow.

---

6. Build a Sustainable Business, Not Just a Job

Too many beauty professionals treat their work as a job rather than a business. They exchange hours for dollars, which limits their income to how much time they can work. This book will teach you how to break free from that cycle by creating a sustainable business that generates income even when you're not working.

You'll learn how to:

- Hire and train employees who uphold your standards.
- Delegate tasks so you can focus on growth.
- Scale your business to multiple locations or franchises.

By thinking like a business owner instead of an employee, you'll unlock unlimited earning potential.

Financial Mastery for Beauty Professionals:
From $0 to Salon Empire

7. Create a Legacy

Success isn't just about making money—it's about creating a lasting impact. This book will help you think beyond yourself, focusing on how you can give back to your community, mentor the next generation of beauty professionals, and leave a legacy that extends far beyond your career.

Whether it's through mentorship, philanthropy, or simply building a business that inspires others, you'll learn how to make your success meaningful.

---

8. Real-Life Examples and Success Stories

This isn't a theoretical book filled with abstract ideas. It's packed with real-life examples of beauty professionals who started with nothing and built thriving businesses. You'll read stories of individuals who faced challenges just like yours and overcame them to achieve financial freedom.

These stories aren't just inspiring—they're practical. They'll show you exactly what's possible and how to make it happen for yourself.

---

9. A Guide Tailored to Beauty Professionals

Financial Mastery for Beauty Professionals:
From $0 to Salon Empire

Most financial advice books aren't written for beauty professionals. They don't understand the unique challenges and opportunities of this industry—seasonal income fluctuations, the importance of client relationships, or the power of creativity in building a brand.

This book is different. It's written specifically for you, with strategies and insights tailored to the beauty industry. It's about empowering you to succeed on your own terms, in a way that aligns with your passion and purpose.

---

10. Take Control of Your Financial Future Today

You can't rely on anyone else to secure your future—not your employer, not the government, and not luck. The responsibility lies with you. But the good news is, you have everything you need to succeed.

This book will give you the tools, knowledge, and confidence to take control of your financial destiny. Whether you're just starting out or looking to take your business to the next level, the principles in this book will guide you every step of the way.

Financial Mastery for Beauty Professionals:
From $0 to Salon Empire

11. A Message of Empowerment

At its core, this book isn't just about money—it's about empowerment. It's about proving to yourself that you're capable of more than you ever imagined. It's about unlocking your full potential, not just as a beauty professional, but as a business owner, leader, and creator of wealth.

---

12. A Roadmap to a Better Life

Imagine a life where you're not worried about money, where you wake up each day excited about what you're building. Imagine having the freedom to pursue your passions, support your loved ones, and give back to your community.

This book is your roadmap to that life. It's not a quick fix or a get-rich-quick scheme—it's a guide to sustainable, long-term success.

Conclusion: Your Journey Starts Now

You picked up this book for a reason. Maybe you're tired of struggling financially. Maybe you want to take your career to the next level. Or maybe you're simply curious about what's possible.

Financial Mastery for Beauty Professionals:
From $0 to Salon Empire

Whatever brought you here, this book is your opportunity to change your life. But remember: knowledge alone isn't enough. It's action that creates results.

So, are you ready to take the first step? Open this book, start reading, and let's build your financial future together.

Financial Mastery for Beauty Professionals:
From $0 to Salon Empire

Contents

Why You Should Read This Book 2

Copyright © 2024 by Di Tran Enterprise 14

Introduction 16

Part 1: Laying the Foundation 24

  Chapter 1: The Beauty Industry as a Launchpad 24

  Chapter 2: The Power of Financial Discipline 32

  Chapter 3: Starting Small: $0 to Something Significant 40

Part 2: Growing Your Business 48

  Chapter 4: From Booth Renter to Business Owner 48

  Chapter 5: Scaling Your Business: From One Salon to Many 58

  Chapter 6: Turning Your Business into a Wealth Engine 68

Part 3: Real Estate as the Cornerstone of Wealth .. 78

  Chapter 7: Mastering Taxes: Turning Expenses into Investments 78

  Chapter 8: The Wealth Mindset: Breaking Emotional Barriers 87

  Chapter 9: Leaving a Legacy: Empowering the Next Generation 96

Financial Mastery for Beauty Professionals:
From $0 to Salon Empire

Part 4: Financial Mastery and Legacy Building 107

   Chapter 10: Creating a Sustainable Financial Foundation 107

   Chapter 11: Balancing Work and Life as a Beauty Professional 117

   Chapter 12: Your Roadmap to Continuous Growth 126

The End 141

Financial Mastery for Beauty Professionals:
From $0 to Salon Empire

Copyright © 2024 by Di Tran Enterprise

All rights reserved. No part of this publication may be reproduced, distributed, or transmitted in any form or by any means, including photocopying, recording, or other electronic or mechanical methods, without the prior written permission of the publisher, except in the case of brief quotations embodied in critical reviews and certain other noncommercial uses permitted by copyright law.

The information contained in this book is intended for educational and inspirational purposes only. It is sold with the understanding that the publisher and author are not engaged in rendering psychological, counseling, or other professional services. If expert assistance is required, the services of a competent professional should be sought.

This publication is designed to provide accurate and authoritative information in regard to the subject matter covered. It is presented with the understanding that the author and publisher are not engaged in rendering personal, professional, or any other kind of advice. The reader should consult his or her medical, legal, financial, or other competent

Financial Mastery for Beauty Professionals:
From $0 to Salon Empire

professional before adopting any of the suggestions in this book or drawing inferences from it.

This publication reflects the author's views, experiences, and opinions. It is intended to provide helpful and informative material on the subjects addressed in the publication. The author and publisher shall have neither liability nor responsibility to any person or entity with respect to any loss, damage, or injury caused, or alleged to be caused, directly or indirectly by the information contained in this book.

While the author has made every effort to ensure the accuracy and completeness of the information contained in this publication, we assume no responsibility for errors, inaccuracies, omissions, or any inconsistency herein. Any slights of people or organizations are unintentional.

Financial Mastery for Beauty Professionals:
From $0 to Salon Empire

Introduction

A Life of Dedication, Discipline, and Financial Mastery

In the beauty industry, success is often measured by the number of clients you serve, the skills you master, and the reputation you build. But for Di Tran, success has always been about something far greater—creating opportunities, building wealth that lasts, and empowering others to achieve their own version of success.

This book is not just a guide to financial management and investment for beauty professionals. It is the culmination of over two decades of relentless hard work, unwavering discipline, and a deep desire to share the lessons learned along the way. My name is Di Tran, and I'm here to walk you through my journey—a journey that started in a high school classroom in Louisville, Kentucky, and has grown into a series of thriving salons, beauty colleges, and real estate investments.

More importantly, this is your journey too. This book is for every beauty professional who dreams of something more, who wants to break free from

Financial Mastery for Beauty Professionals:
From $0 to Salon Empire
paycheck-to-paycheck living, and who is ready to turn their passion into lasting financial freedom.

The Beginning: Balancing Beauty and Education

My story begins at Seneca High School in Louisville, Kentucky, where I was a hardworking 11th-grade student with big dreams and a relentless work ethic. While many of my peers spent their weekends hanging out or relaxing, I spent mine working in salons. At just 16 years old, I earned my nail technician license and began a journey that would shape my life in ways I couldn't have imagined.

From the very beginning, I understood the value of time. While I was pursuing my high school education, I was also working in the beauty industry, serving clients and honing my skills. This wasn't just a part-time job for me—it was the foundation of my future.

College and Beyond: The Balancing Act of a Lifetime

After high school, I pursued a Bachelor's degree in Computer Science and Engineering at the prestigious Speed School of the University of

Financial Mastery for Beauty Professionals:
From $0 to Salon Empire

Louisville. But even as I navigated the demanding curriculum of an engineering program, I never stopped working in salons. I would spend weekdays in classes and weekends driving from salon to salon, often working in multiple locations in a single day to handle a backlog of waiting customers.

Some may have seen this as a grueling schedule, but for me, it was an investment. I was investing in my skills, my reputation, and my financial future. I learned to manage my time and money with precision, knowing that every dollar I earned was a step closer to my goals.

My passion for education didn't stop there. I went on to earn a Master's degree in Computer Science and Engineering from the University of Louisville, and later, a PhD in IT Management from Sullivan University. Throughout it all, I remained deeply rooted in the beauty industry. Working in salons wasn't just a way to make money; it was a way to stay connected to the community, refine my business acumen, and develop a mindset of discipline and perseverance.

The Mindset: Elevating People Through Small Business Ownership

Financial Mastery for Beauty Professionals:
From $0 to Salon Empire

Over the years, I've come to realize that the beauty industry is about so much more than providing services. It's about creating opportunities—for clients to feel confident and for professionals to build lives of purpose and financial freedom.

I've always believed in elevating people to the next level, and for me, that has meant helping others transition from being employees to becoming business owners. The beauty industry is uniquely positioned for this kind of growth. Starting small, as a booth renter or independent contractor, can lead to owning a salon, a chain of salons, and eventually, a thriving real estate portfolio.

This is the journey I've taken, and it's the journey I want to share with you.

Why Real Estate Is the Foundation of Everything

If there's one thing I've learned in my 20+ years in the beauty industry, it's this: all business is ultimately about real estate. At its core, real estate is the only asset that's truly "real." It's tangible, it appreciates over time, and it provides a foundation for long-term wealth.

When you own the building where your salon operates, you're no longer just running a business—

Financial Mastery for Beauty Professionals:
From $0 to Salon Empire

you're building equity. You're creating an asset that can appreciate in value, generate passive income, and provide financial security for years to come.

This philosophy has guided every decision I've made. My salons aren't just places to provide beauty services; they're investments. And as I've expanded into beauty colleges like Louisville Beauty Academy, I've continued to prioritize real estate as the foundation of my enterprise.

The Importance of Financial Discipline

One of the keys to my success has been an unshakable commitment to financial discipline. I've never been one to waste money or spend to satisfy fleeting emotions. Too often, people make financial decisions based on how they feel in the moment—whether it's buying something to feel good, keeping up with trends, or indulging in unnecessary luxuries.

I've taken a different approach. For me, writing, sharing knowledge, and building businesses are what bring me satisfaction. My happiness doesn't come from spending money; it comes from seeing the impact of my work, from helping others succeed, and from watching my investments grow.

Financial Mastery for Beauty Professionals:
From $0 to Salon Empire

This mindset is at the heart of this book. I want to help you develop the same financial discipline and clarity, so you can make decisions that serve your long-term goals—not just your short-term desires.

Why I Wrote This Book

This book is more than a guide to financial management—it's a blueprint for transformation. I wrote it because I've seen too many beauty professionals struggle unnecessarily. They work hard, they're talented, but they don't have the financial knowledge or strategies to turn their efforts into lasting wealth.

My goal is to change that. I want to show you how to:

1. **Start with what you have, no matter how small.** Even if you're starting with $0, you can build something incredible with the right mindset and strategies.

2. **Double your income and investments systematically.** Small, consistent actions can lead to exponential growth.

Financial Mastery for Beauty Professionals:
From $0 to Salon Empire

3. **Transition from employee to entrepreneur.** Learn how to take control of your career by starting your own business.

4. **Invest in real estate.** Understand why owning the property where your business operates is one of the smartest financial moves you can make.

5. **Master financial discipline.** Break free from emotional spending and redirect your money toward opportunities that create real, lasting value.

What You'll Learn

In this book, I'll walk you through every step of the journey:

- **How to start small and scale up.** Whether you're a student, an employee, or a business owner, there's always a way to grow.

- **How to manage your money wisely.** Learn how to budget, invest, and plan for the future.

- **How to create multiple income streams.** From salon services to real estate, I'll show you how to diversify your earnings.

Financial Mastery for Beauty Professionals:
From $0 to Salon Empire

- **How to build a legacy.** This isn't just about making money—it's about creating something that lasts, something that inspires others, and something that leaves a mark.

A Final Note: This Is Your Time

The beauty industry is full of potential. It's an industry where creativity meets opportunity, where hard work can lead to financial independence, and where anyone with the right mindset can succeed.

But success doesn't happen by chance. It happens by choice. It happens when you decide to take control of your finances, invest in your future, and work relentlessly toward your goals.

This book is your guide to making that choice. It's your roadmap to financial mastery, personal growth, and lasting success.

So, are you ready to take the first step? Let's get started.

Financial Mastery for Beauty Professionals:
From $0 to Salon Empire

Part 1: Laying the Foundation

Chapter 1: The Beauty Industry as a Launchpad

Why the Beauty Industry is Unique and Promising

The beauty industry isn't just about haircuts, manicures, and skincare—it's about transformation. It's one of the few industries where creativity, passion, and personal connection are the cornerstones of success. But beyond its artistic side, the beauty industry is a fertile ground for building wealth.

Globally, the beauty industry is valued at hundreds of billions of dollars, and it's growing steadily. People will always prioritize their appearance, making beauty services a resilient and evergreen market. Whether we're in an economic boom or downturn, beauty professionals play an essential role in boosting confidence and self-esteem.

But what sets the beauty industry apart as a launchpad for wealth and entrepreneurship is its accessibility. Unlike many industries, entering the

Financial Mastery for Beauty Professionals:
From $0 to Salon Empire

beauty world doesn't require a massive upfront investment or advanced degrees. With a relatively low barrier to entry, anyone with the determination to succeed can start small and grow big.

How the Beauty Industry Can Build Wealth

1. Low Initial Investment

Starting as a beauty professional often requires minimal upfront costs. A nail technician license, for example, can be obtained for a few thousand dollars or less. Compared to industries that demand years of expensive education or large-scale investment, the beauty industry allows you to start earning almost immediately after completing your training.

2. Scalability

You can begin as an employee in someone else's salon, learn the ropes, and eventually scale up to owning your own business. From there, the opportunities are limitless: booth renting, opening multiple salons, creating your own beauty brand, or even offering training through beauty colleges.

3. Personal Branding and Client Loyalty

Your reputation is your currency in the beauty industry. By offering excellent services and building

Financial Mastery for Beauty Professionals: From $0 to Salon Empire

strong client relationships, you can create a loyal following. Loyal clients not only ensure steady income but can also help you expand your reach through referrals and word-of-mouth marketing.

4. Community and Network Building

The beauty industry is inherently social. Every day, you interact with clients, coworkers, and other professionals. This provides an unparalleled opportunity to network, learn, and grow. These connections can open doors to partnerships, mentorships, and business opportunities.

What You Can Do Right Now

1. Start With Self-Education

Even if you're not yet licensed or working in the industry, you can begin learning today. Research the various beauty fields—nail technology, hair styling, esthetics, or barbering—and choose a path that excites you. Watch online tutorials, read industry blogs, and follow successful professionals on social media.

2. Understand the Financials

Start learning about how money flows in the beauty industry. Ask questions like:

Financial Mastery for Beauty Professionals:
From $0 to Salon Empire

- What does it cost to rent a booth?
- How much can you charge for your services?
- What are the overhead costs of running a salon?

3. Build a Personal Brand

Even as a student or entry-level professional, you can start cultivating your brand. Think about how you want to present yourself to clients. Are you the fun, creative stylist? The reliable, meticulous nail tech? Define your identity and start living it.

4. Practice Client-Centric Behavior

The beauty industry thrives on relationships. Begin practicing active listening, empathy, and excellent customer service skills. These habits will set you apart and ensure clients keep coming back.

Behavior to Foster and Turn Into Habits

1. Always Be Learning

The beauty industry is constantly evolving with new techniques, trends, and products. Commit to lifelong learning by attending workshops, enrolling in advanced courses, and staying updated with

Financial Mastery for Beauty Professionals:
From $0 to Salon Empire

industry news. Make education a non-negotiable habit.

2. Discipline Over Emotion

The key to success in the beauty industry—and in life—is discipline. Avoid making emotional decisions about spending, working, or even interacting with clients. Develop the habit of thinking logically and strategically.

3. Consistency in Service

Clients value reliability. Always deliver high-quality service, regardless of your mood or external circumstances. Consistency builds trust, and trust builds loyalty.

4. Time Management

The beauty industry often involves long hours, especially when you're starting out. Learn to manage your time effectively. Prioritize tasks, stick to a schedule, and always leave room for client interactions.

5. Networking Mindset

Every interaction is an opportunity to build your network. Whether it's a client, coworker, or industry professional, treat everyone as a potential

Financial Mastery for Beauty Professionals:
From $0 to Salon Empire

connection. Make it a habit to exchange ideas, business cards, or social media handles.

Examples of Success: Real-Life Stories

From Nail Tech to Salon Owner

Consider the story of Maria, a nail technician who started working in a small neighborhood salon. Maria was diligent about saving her earnings and reinvesting in her skills. Over five years, she built a loyal client base and eventually rented a booth at a more prominent salon. Within three years of booth renting, she had saved enough to open her own salon. Today, Maria owns three locations and has a growing team of employees.

Building a Personal Brand

Alex, a hairstylist, started by documenting his work on social media. He posted before-and-after photos, tutorials, and client testimonials. By consistently showcasing his skills, Alex attracted a following that extended beyond his immediate client base. When he eventually opened his own salon, clients lined up to book appointments, thanks to the trust and credibility he had built online.

Real Estate as a Foundation

Financial Mastery for Beauty Professionals:
From $0 to Salon Empire

Sarah began her career as an esthetician renting a room in a small spa. She soon realized the value of owning her workspace. With the help of a business loan, Sarah purchased a small building and transformed it into a high-end spa. The property not only houses her business but also generates rental income from other beauty professionals who lease space in her building.

Why You Should Leverage the Beauty Industry Now

The beauty industry is a field where creativity meets opportunity. It's a place where you can start with almost nothing and build a future that's limited only by your imagination and determination. By approaching your career with a strategic mindset, you can leverage the industry to create not just a job, but a thriving business and a foundation for long-term wealth.

But it all starts with taking action. The beauty industry won't wait for you to be ready—you have to dive in, learn as you go, and seize every opportunity.

What's Next?

Financial Mastery for Beauty Professionals:
From $0 to Salon Empire

In the next chapter, we'll dive deeper into **The Power of Financial Discipline**—the cornerstone of turning your passion into profit. You'll learn how to break free from emotional spending, create a solid budget, and redirect your money toward investments that truly matter. Remember, success in the beauty industry isn't just about skill; it's about strategy.

So, let's get started. Your journey to financial freedom and business ownership begins now.

Financial Mastery for Beauty Professionals:
From $0 to Salon Empire

Chapter 2: The Power of Financial Discipline

Why Financial Discipline Matters

Financial discipline is the cornerstone of wealth creation. Without it, even the highest income can slip through your fingers, leaving you stuck in a cycle of paycheck-to-paycheck living. For beauty professionals, this is especially critical. The beauty industry often operates on irregular income, with earnings fluctuating depending on client volume, seasonality, and personal availability.

Financial discipline gives you control. It's the ability to manage money wisely, prioritize investments over fleeting desires, and make decisions that align with your long-term goals. It's about understanding that every dollar is a tool—a seed that, when planted correctly, can grow into a tree of opportunities.

The Emotional Side of Spending

Most people spend money based on emotion. It feels good to buy a new outfit, treat yourself to a nice dinner, or upgrade to the latest beauty tools. However, these emotional decisions often lead to financial stagnation.

Financial Mastery for Beauty Professionals:
From $0 to Salon Empire

Imagine this: You've earned $200 in a day from clients. Instead of saving or reinvesting that money, you spend it on a luxury item you don't truly need. The satisfaction is fleeting, and when an opportunity arises—such as investing in a new business or attending a workshop—you realize you don't have the funds.

Financial discipline is about separating feelings from finances. It's about asking yourself, "Will this expense bring me closer to my goals?" If the answer is no, then it's an emotional indulgence, not an investment.

The Path to Financial Discipline

1. Understand Your Current Financial Habits

The first step to financial discipline is awareness. Track your spending for a month to see where your money goes. Are you spending more than necessary on coffee, clothes, or entertainment? Recognizing patterns is the foundation for change.

2. Create a Budget and Stick to It

A budget is a plan for your money. It ensures that every dollar you earn has a purpose, whether it's for

Financial Mastery for Beauty Professionals:
From $0 to Salon Empire

necessities, savings, or investments. Start with these categories:

- **Necessities:** Rent, utilities, groceries.
- **Business Expenses:** Supplies, booth rent, marketing.
- **Savings and Investments:** Emergency fund, education, retirement.
- **Discretionary Spending:** Entertainment, dining out, luxury items.

3. Build an Emergency Fund

Life is unpredictable. An emergency fund—ideally three to six months of living expenses—acts as a safety net. It prevents you from going into debt when unexpected expenses arise, such as car repairs or medical bills.

4. Pay Yourself First

Before spending a dime on anything else, set aside a portion of your income for savings and investments. This practice, known as "paying yourself first," ensures that you prioritize your future over immediate gratification.

5. Avoid Debt and High-Interest Loans

Financial Mastery for Beauty Professionals:
From $0 to Salon Empire

Debt is a wealth killer. Avoid credit card debt and payday loans, which come with exorbitant interest rates. If you must borrow, do so strategically, such as taking a business loan to purchase real estate or expand your salon.

What You Can Do Right Now

1. Track Your Spending Today

Start by writing down every expense you incur this week. Use a notebook, an app, or a spreadsheet to categorize your spending. This exercise will open your eyes to where your money is going.

2. Set a Savings Goal

Decide on a realistic savings goal for the next three months. For example: "I will save $1,000 for an emergency fund." Break it into smaller, manageable chunks, such as saving $100 per week.

3. Identify One Unnecessary Expense

Look at your spending habits and find one expense you can eliminate or reduce. For example, if you spend $50 a week on dining out, cut it to $25 and redirect the savings to your emergency fund.

4. Create a "No-Spend" Day

Financial Mastery for Beauty Professionals:
From $0 to Salon Empire

Challenge yourself to go one day a week without spending any money. Use this time to reflect on the difference between needs and wants.

Habits to Foster for Financial Discipline

1. Delay Gratification

Practice waiting before making a purchase. If you see something you want, give yourself 24-48 hours to decide if it's truly necessary.

2. Automate Your Savings

Set up automatic transfers from your checking account to a savings or investment account. This ensures consistency and reduces the temptation to spend.

3. Review Your Finances Weekly

Dedicate 30 minutes each week to review your budget, track progress toward your goals, and make adjustments as needed.

4. Celebrate Milestones

When you hit a financial goal, reward yourself in a meaningful but modest way. For example, treat yourself to a small item or experience that aligns with your long-term values.

Financial Mastery for Beauty Professionals:
From $0 to Salon Empire

Examples of Financial Discipline in Action

Jenny: Building an Emergency Fund

Jenny, a hairstylist, realized she was living paycheck to paycheck despite earning a decent income. She started tracking her spending and discovered she was spending $200 a month on unnecessary subscriptions and takeout. Jenny canceled the subscriptions, cut back on takeout, and redirected the money to a savings account. Within six months, she had saved $1,200 for emergencies.

Carlos: Investing in Education

Carlos, a nail technician, wanted to expand his skills to include nail art and advanced techniques. Instead of taking out a loan, Carlos saved $50 a week for six months. He used the $1,200 he saved to attend a workshop, which allowed him to charge higher prices and attract more clients.

Lina: From Debt to Wealth

Lina, a salon owner, was struggling with credit card debt. She created a strict budget, cut unnecessary expenses, and focused on paying off the card with the highest interest rate first. After two years, Lina

Financial Mastery for Beauty Professionals:
From $0 to Salon Empire

was debt-free and used the money she had been spending on interest to invest in real estate.

The Long-Term Benefits of Financial Discipline

1. Freedom from Stress

Money problems are one of the biggest sources of stress. Financial discipline gives you peace of mind, knowing that you're prepared for emergencies and on track to achieve your goals.

2. The Ability to Seize Opportunities

When you manage your money wisely, you're ready to take advantage of opportunities—whether it's investing in a business, buying property, or attending a career-changing workshop.

3. Financial Independence

The ultimate goal of financial discipline is independence. It's about creating a life where you're not reliant on others, where you control your finances, and where your money works for you.

Why Financial Discipline is Non-Negotiable

Financial Mastery for Beauty Professionals:
From $0 to Salon Empire

The beauty industry is full of talented professionals who never reach their potential—not because they lack skill, but because they lack financial discipline. Don't let that be you. You have the power to create a future that's not just financially stable but abundant.

Remember, financial discipline isn't about deprivation—it's about direction. It's about making choices today that align with the life you want tomorrow.

What's Next?

In the next chapter, we'll explore **Starting Small: $0 to Something Significant.** You'll learn how to double your money step by step, build momentum, and create the foundation for lasting success.

Your journey to financial freedom starts with discipline. Take the first step today, and let's keep moving forward.

Financial Mastery for Beauty Professionals:
From $0 to Salon Empire

Chapter 3: Starting Small: $0 to Something Significant

Why Starting Small is Powerful

Many people hesitate to pursue their dreams because they believe they need significant resources to get started. They think they need thousands of dollars, the perfect tools, or a fully established business plan before they can begin. This couldn't be further from the truth.

The most successful businesses and careers often start small. Starting small isn't a limitation—it's a strength. It allows you to experiment, learn, and grow without taking on overwhelming risks. By starting with what you have and doubling your efforts over time, you can create something extraordinary.

The beauty industry is the perfect example of how small beginnings can lead to significant success. Whether you're working as a nail technician, hairstylist, esthetician, or makeup artist, you can start with minimal resources and gradually scale up your income, skills, and business.

The Why: The Compound Effect of Small Steps

Financial Mastery for Beauty Professionals:
From $0 to Salon Empire

The principle of starting small is rooted in the compound effect. Small, consistent actions, when repeated over time, lead to exponential growth. For example:

- If you save $10 a week, you'll have $520 at the end of the year.
- If you add just one new client a week, that's 52 additional clients in a year.
- If you reinvest your earnings into better tools or education, you can charge higher rates and attract more clients.

The key is to take the first step, no matter how small, and stay consistent.

The How: Practical Steps to Start Small

1. Start Where You Are

You don't need the latest tools or a fancy setup to begin. Use what you already have and focus on providing excellent service. For example:

- If you're a nail technician, invest in basic tools and gradually upgrade as you earn more.
- If you're a hairstylist, start by offering services to friends and family before renting a booth.

Financial Mastery for Beauty Professionals:
From $0 to Salon Empire

2. Focus on Doubling

The concept of doubling is simple yet powerful. Start with a small amount, like $1, and focus on doubling it:

- Use your first earnings to buy better supplies.
- Use improved tools to attract more clients and increase your rates.
- Reinvest your profits into marketing, education, or additional services.

3. Offer Affordable Services to Build Momentum

When you're starting, prioritize volume over profit. Offer discounted rates or promotions to attract clients. Once you've built a loyal client base, you can gradually increase your prices.

4. Network Relentlessly

Success in the beauty industry relies heavily on word-of-mouth and relationships. Attend local events, collaborate with other professionals, and always carry business cards or social media links.

5. Save and Reinvest

Instead of spending your earnings on unnecessary items, reinvest them into your business. For example:

Financial Mastery for Beauty Professionals:
From $0 to Salon Empire

- Save for advanced courses to improve your skills.
- Purchase better tools or equipment.
- Invest in marketing to attract more clients.

What You Can Do Right Now

1. Identify Your Starting Point

Ask yourself: What can I do with what I have right now? Write down your available resources, such as skills, tools, and connections.

2. Set a Small, Achievable Goal

Start with a simple goal, like earning an extra $100 this month or gaining three new clients. Break it down into actionable steps.

3. Take Action Today

Don't wait for the perfect moment—take action now. Post your services on social media, reach out to potential clients, or offer free or discounted services to friends and family.

4. Track Your Progress

Financial Mastery for Beauty Professionals:
From $0 to Salon Empire

Keep a record of your income, expenses, and client growth. Seeing your progress will motivate you to keep going.

Behavior to Foster and Turn Into Habits

1. Consistency is Key

Make small, consistent actions a daily habit. Whether it's practicing your skills, reaching out to clients, or saving money, consistency compounds over time.

2. Celebrate Small Wins

Every milestone, no matter how small, is worth celebrating. It reinforces your progress and motivates you to keep going.

3. Stay Resourceful

Develop the habit of making the most of what you have. Instead of focusing on what you lack, find creative ways to maximize your resources.

4. Reinvest Automatically

Whenever you earn money, set aside a portion for reinvestment. Treat this as a non-negotiable habit.

Financial Mastery for Beauty Professionals:
From $0 to Salon Empire
Examples of Success: Real-Life Stories

Sophia: The Nail Technician Who Doubled Her Way to Success

Sophia started her career with a basic nail kit she purchased for $50. She offered discounted services to friends and family and reinvested her earnings into better tools. Within a year, she had built a loyal client base and was earning enough to rent a booth at a local salon. Today, Sophia owns her own salon and has a team of nail technicians working under her.

David: Building a Client Base from Scratch

David, a hairstylist, began his career by offering free haircuts to his neighbors. Word quickly spread, and he started charging a small fee. David reinvested his earnings into marketing and professional development courses. Within two years, he was running a successful salon with a six-figure income.

Linh: Turning Weekend Work into a Thriving Business

Linh worked as an esthetician on weekends while attending college. She saved her earnings and used them to rent a small studio. Linh focused on providing exceptional service, which helped her

Financial Mastery for Beauty Professionals:
From $0 to Salon Empire

attract a steady stream of clients. Today, she owns a chain of skincare clinics.

What Makes Starting Small Sustainable

Starting small is sustainable because it reduces risk. You're not taking on massive debt or making high-stakes investments. Instead, you're building a solid foundation one step at a time.

This approach also gives you the flexibility to learn and adapt. If something doesn't work, you can pivot without significant losses. Starting small allows you to experiment, refine your strategies, and grow at a manageable pace.

Why This Approach Works

The beauty industry is full of opportunities, but it's also highly competitive. Starting small allows you to carve out your niche and establish yourself without overwhelming yourself financially or emotionally.

More importantly, starting small fosters a growth mindset. It teaches you to value progress over perfection, focus on the process, and embrace the journey.

Financial Mastery for Beauty Professionals:
From $0 to Salon Empire

The Long-Term Vision

By starting small and scaling gradually, you're not just building a business—you're building a legacy. Every dollar you earn and reinvest is a step toward financial freedom and independence.

Remember, every successful salon owner, beauty college founder, or real estate investor started somewhere. Their journey began with a single client, a single service, or a single dollar. Your journey can start today, right where you are.

What's Next?

In the next chapter, we'll explore **From Booth Renter to Business Owner**. You'll learn how to transition from working for someone else to becoming your own boss, the financial considerations involved, and the steps to set yourself up for success.

Success starts small, but it doesn't stay small. Let's take the next step together.

Financial Mastery for Beauty Professionals:
From $0 to Salon Empire

Part 2: Growing Your Business

Chapter 4: From Booth Renter to Business Owner

Why Transitioning to Business Ownership Matters

As a beauty professional, renting a booth is often the first step toward independence. It gives you the freedom to manage your schedule, build your client base, and develop your personal brand. However, booth renting has its limitations. While it allows you to keep a larger share of your earnings, you're still working within someone else's space, under someone else's rules, and without building long-term equity.

Transitioning to business ownership is the next logical step for those who want more control, more income potential, and the ability to create a lasting legacy. Owning your salon not only increases your earning potential but also allows you to shape the environment, services, and culture of your business. It's a step toward true independence and long-term wealth.

Financial Mastery for Beauty Professionals:
From $0 to Salon Empire

The Why: Benefits of Owning Your Salon

1. Increased Earning Potential

As a booth renter, you earn based on the services you provide. As a salon owner, you can generate additional income by renting booths or hiring employees. Every chair, every stylist, and every service contributes to your bottom line.

2. Control Over the Environment

Owning your salon gives you complete control over its atmosphere, branding, and operations. You can create a space that reflects your vision and attracts your ideal clientele.

3. Building Equity

When you own the building your salon operates in, you're not just running a business—you're building equity in a valuable asset. Real estate ownership transforms your salon into an investment that appreciates over time.

4. Legacy Building

Owning a salon allows you to create something that lasts. Whether it's passing the business to your

Financial Mastery for Beauty Professionals:
From $0 to Salon Empire

children or selling it for a profit, you're building a legacy that goes beyond your day-to-day work.

The How: Steps to Transition from Booth Renter to Business Owner

1. Assess Your Readiness

Before making the leap, evaluate whether you're ready for the responsibilities of ownership. Consider these questions:

- Do you have a loyal client base?
- Have you saved enough to cover startup costs?
- Are you prepared to manage employees, finances, and operations?

2. Develop a Business Plan

A solid business plan is essential for securing funding, attracting clients, and guiding your operations. Your plan should include:

- A description of your services and target market.
- Financial projections, including startup costs and expected income.

Financial Mastery for Beauty Professionals:
From $0 to Salon Empire

- A marketing strategy to attract and retain clients.
- Operational details, such as hours of operation, staffing, and supplies.

3. Save and Secure Funding

Starting a salon requires an initial investment for space, equipment, and supplies. Begin saving early and explore funding options such as:

- Personal savings.
- Small business loans.
- Partnerships or investors.

4. Choose the Right Location

Location is critical to your salon's success. Consider factors like foot traffic, parking availability, and proximity to your target audience.

5. Design Your Space

The design of your salon should reflect your brand and create a welcoming atmosphere for clients. Focus on functionality, comfort, and aesthetics.

6. Hire and Train a Team

As a salon owner, your team is your greatest asset. Hire skilled professionals who align with your values

Financial Mastery for Beauty Professionals:
From $0 to Salon Empire

and vision. Provide ongoing training to ensure consistent service quality.

7. Market Your Salon

Develop a marketing strategy to promote your salon. This can include:

- Creating a professional website.
- Using social media to showcase your work.
- Offering promotions to attract new clients.

What You Can Do Right Now

1. Start Saving

If you're currently a booth renter, begin setting aside a portion of your income for future salon ownership. Aim to save enough to cover at least three to six months of operating expenses.

2. Research Local Market Conditions

Investigate the demand for salons in your area. Look at your competitors, their pricing, and their services. Identify gaps in the market that your salon can fill.

3. Build Your Brand

Financial Mastery for Beauty Professionals:
From $0 to Salon Empire

Even before owning a salon, start establishing your brand identity. Create a logo, choose a color scheme, and maintain a consistent online presence.

4. Strengthen Client Relationships

Your existing clients will be your biggest supporters when you open your salon. Focus on building strong, loyal relationships by providing exceptional service.

Habits to Foster for a Successful Transition

1. Financial Discipline

Owning a salon requires significant financial investment. Cultivate the habit of saving and managing your money wisely.

2. Leadership Skills

As a salon owner, you'll need to lead a team. Practice effective communication, decision-making, and problem-solving.

3. Continuous Learning

The beauty industry is always evolving. Stay ahead of trends by attending workshops, networking with other professionals, and investing in education.

Financial Mastery for Beauty Professionals:
From $0 to Salon Empire

4. Customer-Centric Mindset

Happy clients are the foundation of a successful salon. Make it a habit to prioritize their needs and exceed their expectations.

Examples of Success: Real-Life Stories

Emma: From Booth Renter to Multi-Salon Owner

Emma started her career renting a booth in a local salon. She saved a portion of her income every month and eventually secured a small business loan to open her own salon. Emma focused on creating a unique client experience, and her salon quickly gained popularity. Today, Emma owns three salons and is mentoring other beauty professionals.

James: Turning a Vision into Reality

James, a barber, spent years building a loyal client base as a booth renter. He saw an opportunity to create a modern barbershop that catered to young professionals. With a clear vision and meticulous planning, James opened his first shop. Within five years, he had expanded to four locations, each designed to reflect his brand's sleek and professional image.

Maria: Building a Legacy

Financial Mastery for Beauty Professionals:
From $0 to Salon Empire

Maria worked as a hairstylist for over a decade before opening her salon. She used her experience to create a space that prioritized customer service and community engagement. Maria's salon became a local favorite, and she later purchased the building to secure her investment. Today, Maria's salon is a family business, with her children involved in its operations.

Overcoming Challenges as a Salon Owner

1. Managing Finances

Owning a salon comes with additional expenses, including rent, utilities, and employee salaries. Stay on top of your finances by maintaining a detailed budget and tracking expenses.

2. Balancing Responsibilities

As a salon owner, you'll juggle multiple roles—manager, marketer, and stylist. Learn to delegate tasks and prioritize effectively.

3. Attracting and Retaining Clients

Competition in the beauty industry is fierce. Differentiate your salon by offering exceptional service, creating a unique atmosphere, and regularly engaging with clients through marketing.

Financial Mastery for Beauty Professionals:
From $0 to Salon Empire

4. Navigating Legal and Regulatory Requirements

Ensure your salon complies with local laws and regulations, including licensing, health codes, and employment laws.

The Long-Term Vision

Transitioning from booth renter to salon owner is about more than increasing your income. It's about creating a business that reflects your values, supports your community, and provides a foundation for future growth.

Owning a salon is also a stepping stone to other opportunities, such as opening additional locations, starting a beauty college, or investing in real estate. By taking this step, you're setting yourself up for a lifetime of financial independence and professional fulfillment.

What's Next?

In the next chapter, we'll dive into **Scaling Your Business: From One Salon to Many**. You'll learn how to expand your operations, manage multiple locations, and create a scalable business model.

Financial Mastery for Beauty Professionals:
From $0 to Salon Empire

Your journey to ownership is a powerful step, but it's only the beginning. Let's build something incredible together.

Financial Mastery for Beauty Professionals:
From $0 to Salon Empire

Chapter 5: Scaling Your Business: From One Salon to Many

Why Scaling Matters

Owning one salon is a significant achievement, but for those with bigger ambitions, scaling to multiple locations is the next step. Scaling isn't just about increasing your income—it's about multiplying your impact, creating more opportunities for others, and building a brand that stands out in the beauty industry.

Scaling allows you to expand your reach, serve more clients, and generate additional revenue streams. It's a chance to move from working *in* your business to working *on* it, focusing on strategy and growth rather than daily operations.

The Why: Benefits of Scaling Your Salon Business

1. Increased Revenue Potential

Each additional salon represents a new income stream. By opening multiple locations, you can significantly increase your earning potential while diversifying your revenue sources.

Financial Mastery for Beauty Professionals:
From $0 to Salon Empire

2. Brand Recognition

Scaling your business helps establish your brand as a trusted name in the beauty industry. A well-known brand attracts loyal clients, talented professionals, and potential investors.

3. Economies of Scale

With multiple locations, you can take advantage of bulk purchasing for supplies, shared marketing costs, and streamlined operations, reducing overall expenses.

4. Opportunity to Mentor and Empower Others

Scaling your business creates opportunities to mentor other beauty professionals, giving them a platform to grow while contributing to the success of your brand.

The How: Steps to Scale Your Salon Business

1. Build a Strong Foundation

Before scaling, ensure your first salon is profitable and running smoothly. A solid foundation is essential for sustainable growth. Ask yourself:

- Is my current salon consistently profitable?

Financial Mastery for Beauty Professionals:
From $0 to Salon Empire

- Do I have systems in place for operations, marketing, and client management?
- Am I ready to delegate responsibilities?

2. Develop a Scalable Business Model

A scalable business model is one that can be replicated across multiple locations without compromising quality. Key components include:

- **Standardized Services:** Ensure that every location offers the same high-quality experience.
- **Operational Systems:** Document processes for hiring, training, inventory management, and client service.
- **Strong Branding:** Maintain consistency in your branding, from logo design to social media presence.

3. Research New Locations

Choose locations strategically. Factors to consider include:

- Proximity to your target audience.
- Competition in the area.
- Accessibility and visibility of the location.

Financial Mastery for Beauty Professionals:
From $0 to Salon Empire

4. Secure Funding for Expansion

Scaling requires capital for leases, equipment, hiring, and marketing. Explore funding options such as:

- Profits from your first salon.
- Small business loans or grants.
- Partnerships or investors.

5. Build a Leadership Team

As your business grows, you can't be everywhere at once. Identify and train managers who share your vision and can oversee daily operations at each location.

6. Leverage Technology

Technology can streamline your operations and improve efficiency. Invest in:

- **Point-of-Sale (POS) Systems:** For tracking sales and managing appointments.
- **Customer Relationship Management (CRM) Tools:** To maintain client records and communication.
- **Marketing Platforms:** For social media management and email campaigns.

Financial Mastery for Beauty Professionals:
From $0 to Salon Empire

7. Test and Optimize

Start small by opening one additional location before expanding further. Use this opportunity to identify challenges, test new strategies, and refine your processes.

What You Can Do Right Now

1. Evaluate Your Current Salon

Take a close look at your current salon's performance. Identify areas for improvement and ensure that it's operating at its full potential.

2. Create an Expansion Plan

Write down your vision for scaling your business. Include details about potential locations, target markets, and the steps you need to take to get there.

3. Start Building Your Team

Identify potential leaders within your current team who could take on managerial roles in new locations. Begin training them for future responsibilities.

4. Save for Expansion

Financial Mastery for Beauty Professionals:
From $0 to Salon Empire

Set aside a portion of your profits to fund your next location. Start small, and build your expansion fund over time.

Habits to Foster for Successful Scaling

1. Delegation

Scaling requires you to step back from daily operations and focus on strategy. Learn to trust your team and delegate tasks effectively.

2. Adaptability

Every new location will come with its own challenges. Develop the habit of staying flexible and open to change.

3. Data-Driven Decision Making

Track key performance indicators (KPIs) such as revenue, client retention, and employee satisfaction. Use this data to guide your decisions.

4. Consistent Branding

Ensure that every location reflects your brand's identity. Develop the habit of regularly auditing your marketing materials, social media, and in-salon experience.

Financial Mastery for Beauty Professionals:
From $0 to Salon Empire

Examples of Success: Real-Life Stories

Case Study 1: Maria's Beauty Empire

Maria started with a single salon in a suburban neighborhood. After perfecting her operations and building a strong client base, she opened a second location in a nearby city. Maria standardized her services, hired a manager for each location, and used social media to market her brand. Today, she owns five salons and employs over 50 beauty professionals.

Case Study 2: David's Barber Shops

David, a barber, focused on creating a unique client experience in his first shop. He reinvested his profits into opening a second location near a college campus. By targeting different demographics and offering tailored services, David scaled his business to three barber shops, each catering to a specific audience.

Case Study 3: Lisa's Salon and Spa Chain

Lisa combined her passion for beauty and wellness by creating a salon and spa hybrid. She used her first location to test various services and pricing models. Once she found the right mix, Lisa

Financial Mastery for Beauty Professionals:
From $0 to Salon Empire

expanded to three locations, each offering consistent services with slight variations based on local demand.

Common Challenges in Scaling and How to Overcome Them

1. Maintaining Quality

Challenge: Ensuring consistent service quality across multiple locations.
Solution: Develop detailed training programs and implement quality control measures.

2. Managing Finances

Challenge: Balancing the costs of expansion with existing operations.
Solution: Create a detailed budget for each location and monitor expenses closely.

3. Attracting and Retaining Talent

Challenge: Finding skilled professionals to staff your new locations.
Solution: Offer competitive compensation, invest in employee development, and create a positive work culture.

4. Managing Growth

Financial Mastery for Beauty Professionals:
From $0 to Salon Empire

Challenge: Juggling the demands of multiple locations.

Solution: Use technology to streamline operations and hire a leadership team to oversee day-to-day tasks.

The Long-Term Vision: Scaling Beyond Salons

Scaling doesn't have to stop at multiple salon locations. Once you've mastered the art of expansion, you can explore additional opportunities, such as:

- **Starting a Beauty College:** Share your knowledge and train the next generation of beauty professionals.

- **Creating a Product Line:** Develop your own line of beauty products, from hair care to skincare.

- **Investing in Real Estate:** Purchase properties for your salons and generate additional income through rentals.

Why Scaling Is Worth It

Financial Mastery for Beauty Professionals:
From $0 to Salon Empire

Scaling your business is about more than making money—it's about creating opportunities for yourself, your team, and your community. It's about building a brand that stands the test of time and leaves a lasting impact.

The journey won't be easy, but with careful planning, disciplined execution, and a commitment to excellence, you can achieve incredible success.

What's Next?

In the next chapter, we'll explore **Turning Your Business into a Wealth Engine**. You'll learn how to leverage your salons, diversify your income streams, and build wealth that works for you.

Your dream of expanding your business is within reach. Let's take the next step together.

Financial Mastery for Beauty Professionals:
From $0 to Salon Empire

Chapter 6: Turning Your Business into a Wealth Engine

Why Your Salon Business Should Be More Than a Job

For many beauty professionals, the goal of owning a salon starts with a desire for independence and control. But owning a salon can be so much more than just a means of self-employment—it can be a wealth engine. A wealth engine is a business that generates income beyond what you earn from your direct efforts. It creates passive income, builds equity, and allows you to scale your earnings exponentially.

To turn your salon into a wealth engine, you need to think beyond day-to-day operations. This involves leveraging your business to generate multiple income streams, investing in assets that grow in value, and structuring your finances to work smarter, not harder.

The Why: Benefits of a Wealth Engine

1. Financial Security

A wealth engine generates consistent income, even during economic downturns or personal challenges.

Financial Mastery for Beauty Professionals:
From $0 to Salon Empire

It ensures financial stability for you, your family, and your team.

2. Freedom of Time

When your business is set up to generate passive income, you're no longer tied to working every day. This freedom allows you to focus on strategic growth or enjoy more personal time.

3. Long-Term Wealth Building

A wealth engine focuses on assets like real estate, intellectual property, and investments that appreciate over time, securing your financial future.

4. Scalable Success

By creating systems and diversifying income streams, you can grow your wealth exponentially, rather than being limited by the hours you can personally work.

The How: Turning Your Salon into a Wealth Engine

1. Build Passive Income Streams

Your salon business can generate income beyond the services you directly provide. Examples include:

Financial Mastery for Beauty Professionals:
From $0 to Salon Empire

- **Booth Rentals:** Lease chairs or spaces to independent stylists, nail techs, or estheticians.

- **Retail Sales:** Sell beauty products such as hair care, skincare, or makeup. Choose high-quality brands and train your team to recommend them to clients.

- **Membership Programs:** Offer memberships for discounted services, encouraging repeat business and consistent cash flow.

2. Invest in Real Estate

Owning the property where your salon operates transforms rent into equity. Over time, the property appreciates in value, adding to your wealth. Additionally, you can:

- Lease extra space to other businesses or professionals.

- Invest in additional properties for future salons.

- Use real estate as collateral for loans to expand your business.

3. Create a Scalable Business Model

Financial Mastery for Beauty Professionals:
From $0 to Salon Empire

Develop systems and processes that allow your business to run smoothly without your constant involvement. This includes:

- Standardized training for employees.
- Automated scheduling and payment systems.
- Clear operational procedures for every aspect of your business.

4. Expand Services and Offerings

Diversify your salon's revenue by adding new services or products. For example:

- Introduce high-demand treatments like lash extensions or microblading.
- Offer premium services, such as bridal packages or spa treatments.
- Partner with other businesses to cross-promote services.

5. Focus on Branding and Marketing

A strong brand attracts clients, employees, and investors. Invest in:

- Professional branding, including a logo, webslte, and social media presence.

Financial Mastery for Beauty Professionals:
From $0 to Salon Empire

- Consistent marketing campaigns to build awareness and attract new clients.
- Partnerships with influencers or local businesses to expand your reach.

6. Manage Finances Strategically

Reinvest a portion of your profits into growth opportunities, such as:

- Expanding to new locations.
- Upgrading equipment and facilities.
- Marketing campaigns to attract more clients.

What You Can Do Right Now

1. Identify Passive Income Opportunities

Take a close look at your salon's operations. Are there opportunities to introduce passive income streams, such as retail sales or booth rentals?

2. Evaluate Real Estate Options

If you're currently renting your salon space, research the cost of purchasing property in your area. Start saving for a down payment or exploring financing options.

Financial Mastery for Beauty Professionals:
From $0 to Salon Empire

selling online. Carlos now operates a successful e-commerce business in addition to running his salon.

Maya: Membership Success

Maya introduced a membership program at her spa, offering clients unlimited monthly facials for a fixed fee. The program provided consistent cash flow, increased client retention, and helped Maya expand her services to include more premium treatments.

Challenges of Turning a Business into a Wealth Engine

1. Managing Cash Flow

Challenge: Scaling your business requires significant investment.
Solution: Maintain a detailed budget, monitor cash flow closely, and avoid overextending yourself financially.

2. Maintaining Quality Across Revenue Streams

Challenge: Expanding services or products can dilute your brand if not executed well.
Solution: Focus on quality over quantity. Introduce new offerings gradually and ensure they align with your brand's standards.

Financial Mastery for Beauty Professionals:
From $0 to Salon Empire

3. Balancing Risk and Reward

Challenge: Investing in real estate or new ventures comes with risks.
Solution: Conduct thorough research, seek professional advice, and start small to minimize risk.

Why It's Worth It

Transforming your salon into a wealth engine is about creating a business that works for you—not the other way around. It's about achieving financial freedom, building a legacy, and making a lasting impact on your community.

With careful planning, strategic investments, and a commitment to excellence, your salon can become a powerful tool for wealth creation.

What's Next?

In the next chapter, we'll explore **Mastering Taxes: Turning Expenses into Investments**. You'll learn how to optimize your tax strategy, structure your finances for growth, and keep more of what you earn.

Financial Mastery for Beauty Professionals:
From $0 to Salon Empire

Your salon is more than a job—it's a gateway to financial freedom. Let's take the next step in building your wealth engine.

Financial Mastery for Beauty Professionals:
From $0 to Salon Empire

Part 3: Real Estate as the Cornerstone of Wealth

Chapter 7: Mastering Taxes: Turning Expenses into Investments

Why Taxes Matter for Wealth Building

Taxes are often seen as a burden, but when approached strategically, they can become a powerful tool for building wealth. For beauty professionals, understanding and managing taxes isn't just about compliance—it's about maximizing your income, reinvesting in your business, and keeping more of what you earn.

As a salon owner or beauty professional, you're not just an individual taxpayer; you're a business owner. This gives you access to a range of tax benefits and deductions that can significantly reduce your taxable income. By mastering taxes, you can turn what might feel like a financial drain into an opportunity for growth.

The Why: Benefits of Tax Mastery

1. Reduce Tax Liability

Financial Mastery for Beauty Professionals:
From $0 to Salon Empire

Proper tax planning allows you to take advantage of deductions, credits, and strategies that lower the amount you owe.

2. Increase Cash Flow

Keeping more money in your business means you have more to invest in growth, whether it's expanding your services, upgrading equipment, or hiring staff.

3. Build Long-Term Wealth

Strategic tax planning can free up funds to invest in real estate, retirement accounts, or other wealth-building opportunities.

4. Ensure Compliance and Avoid Penalties

Understanding your tax obligations helps you avoid costly mistakes that could lead to audits, fines, or other legal issues.

The How: Key Tax Strategies for Beauty Professionals

1. Separate Personal and Business Finances

Mixing personal and business expenses is a common mistake among beauty professionals. Open a separate business bank account and credit card to

Financial Mastery for Beauty Professionals:
From $0 to Salon Empire

keep your finances organized. This makes it easier to track expenses, calculate deductions, and prepare for tax season.

2. Take Advantage of Deductions

As a beauty professional, you can deduct many of the expenses related to your work. Common deductions include:

- **Supplies and Equipment:** Nail tools, hair dryers, chairs, etc.
- **Rent and Utilities:** Booth rental or salon lease, electricity, water, and internet.
- **Education and Training:** Workshops, courses, and certifications.
- **Marketing:** Website design, social media ads, and promotional materials.
- **Travel and Mileage:** Travel expenses for attending industry events or serving clients off-site.
- **Uniforms and Professional Clothing:** Clothing or uniforms required for work.

3. Maximize Depreciation

If you've invested in expensive equipment or property, you can deduct a portion of the cost each

Financial Mastery for Beauty Professionals:
From $0 to Salon Empire

year through depreciation. This reduces your taxable income while reflecting the gradual wear and tear of your assets.

4. Use the Home Office Deduction

If you work from home or have a designated space for managing your business, you may qualify for a home office deduction. This allows you to deduct a portion of your rent, mortgage, utilities, and maintenance costs.

5. Contribute to a Retirement Account

As a self-employed professional, you have access to retirement accounts like a SEP IRA or a Solo 401(k). Contributions to these accounts are tax-deductible and help you build long-term wealth.

6. Track Mileage and Travel Expenses

If you travel to clients, purchase supplies, or attend industry events, you can deduct the associated mileage and travel costs. Use a mileage tracker app to record your trips accurately.

7. Hire a Professional

While it's important to understand the basics of tax management, working with a tax professional or accountant ensures you're maximizing deductions and complying with regulations.

Financial Mastery for Beauty Professionals:
From $0 to Salon Empire

What You Can Do Right Now

1. Organize Your Finances

Set up a separate business bank account and credit card if you haven't already. This simplifies record-keeping and makes it easier to identify deductible expenses.

2. Start Tracking Expenses

Keep detailed records of all your business-related expenses. Use accounting software or a simple spreadsheet to categorize your spending.

3. Research Deductions

Familiarize yourself with the deductions available to beauty professionals. Make a list of expenses you regularly incur and check if they're tax-deductible.

4. Plan for Quarterly Taxes

If you're self-employed, you're responsible for paying estimated taxes quarterly. Set aside a portion of your income each month to cover these payments.

Habits to Foster for Tax Mastery

Financial Mastery for Beauty Professionals:
From $0 to Salon Empire

1. Maintain Detailed Records

Make it a habit to save receipts, invoices, and other financial documents. Accurate records are essential for claiming deductions and surviving an audit.

2. Review Finances Monthly

Dedicate time each month to review your income, expenses, and tax obligations. This keeps you informed and prepared.

3. Stay Educated

Tax laws change frequently. Keep up with updates that affect your industry by following reputable sources or consulting a tax professional.

4. Automate Savings for Taxes

Set up an automatic transfer to a separate savings account for taxes. Aim to save 20-30% of your income to cover estimated tax payments.

Examples of Success: Real-Life Stories

Case Study 1: Julia's Journey to Tax Savings

Julia, a nail technician, used to dread tax season. She often mixed personal and business expenses, leaving her overwhelmed and unprepared. After

Financial Mastery for Beauty Professionals:
From $0 to Salon Empire

consulting with a tax professional, Julia set up a separate business account and started tracking her expenses. She discovered she could deduct her mileage, supplies, and booth rental costs. That year, Julia saved over $5,000 in taxes.

Case Study 2: David's Real Estate Advantage

David, a salon owner, decided to purchase the property where his salon was located. By working with his accountant, he learned about depreciation and interest deductions, which significantly reduced his taxable income. Over five years, David built equity in the property while saving thousands in taxes.

Case Study 3: Anna's Retirement Plan

Anna, a hairstylist, opened a SEP IRA and began contributing 10% of her income. Not only did this reduce her taxable income, but it also gave her peace of mind knowing she was building a retirement fund.

Common Challenges and How to Overcome Them

1. Lack of Organization

Financial Mastery for Beauty Professionals:
From $0 to Salon Empire

Challenge: Many beauty professionals struggle to keep track of expenses and income.

Solution: Use accounting software or hire a bookkeeper to stay organized.

2. Missing Deadlines

Challenge: Forgetting to pay quarterly taxes or file returns on time.

Solution: Set calendar reminders and automate payments whenever possible.

3. Overlooking Deductions

Challenge: Failing to claim all eligible deductions.

Solution: Work with a tax professional who understands the beauty industry.

The Long-Term Vision: Using Taxes to Build Wealth

Mastering taxes isn't just about saving money—it's about using those savings to invest in your future. Whether it's purchasing property, funding your retirement, or expanding your business, the money you save on taxes can be redirected toward wealth-building opportunities.

Financial Mastery for Beauty Professionals:
From $0 to Salon Empire

By approaching taxes strategically, you're not just complying with the law—you're turning a financial obligation into a tool for growth.

Why It's Worth It

Taxes are one of the biggest expenses for any business, but they don't have to be a burden. With the right knowledge and strategies, you can minimize your liability, maximize your savings, and create a solid foundation for long-term success.

What's Next?

In the next chapter, we'll explore **The Wealth Mindset: Breaking Emotional Barriers.** You'll learn how to overcome limiting beliefs about money, develop habits for financial success, and cultivate a mindset that supports your long-term goals.

Taxes don't have to be intimidating. Let's turn them into one of your greatest financial advantages.

Financial Mastery for Beauty Professionals:
From $0 to Salon Empire

Chapter 8: The Wealth Mindset: Breaking Emotional Barriers

Why Your Mindset Matters

Wealth is not just about money—it's about mindset. You can have all the financial tools, strategies, and resources in the world, but without the right mindset, you'll struggle to make meaningful progress.

For beauty professionals, breaking emotional barriers is especially important. Many of us come from humble beginnings, carrying beliefs about money that can hold us back. Whether it's fear of failure, guilt about earning more, or a tendency to overspend emotionally, these barriers can prevent us from reaching our full potential.

Cultivating a wealth mindset means seeing money as a tool for growth, not as something to fear or chase. It's about focusing on abundance, building positive habits, and believing in your ability to succeed.

The Why: Benefits of a Wealth Mindset

1. Overcoming Fear and Limiting Beliefs

A wealth mindset helps you move past fears like:

Financial Mastery for Beauty Professionals:
From $0 to Salon Empire

- "I'm not good with money."
- "I don't deserve to earn more."
- "What if I fail?"

These thoughts can paralyze you, but with the right mindset, you'll have the confidence to take action.

2. Building Resilience

A wealth mindset keeps you focused on long-term goals, even when you face setbacks. It helps you see challenges as opportunities to learn and grow.

3. Encouraging Discipline and Focus

When you adopt a wealth mindset, you become intentional about how you spend, save, and invest. You prioritize actions that align with your goals.

4. Creating a Vision for Success

A positive mindset allows you to envision what's possible and take the necessary steps to turn your dreams into reality.

The How: Steps to Develop a Wealth Mindset

1. Identify and Challenge Limiting Beliefs

Financial Mastery for Beauty Professionals:
From $0 to Salon Empire

Many of us grow up with beliefs about money that don't serve us, such as:

- "Money is the root of all evil."
- "Rich people are greedy."
- "I'll never have enough."

Write down your beliefs about money and examine where they came from. Ask yourself: Are these beliefs true? Replace them with empowering thoughts, like:

- "Money is a tool to create opportunities."
- "I deserve financial success."
- "I have the skills and determination to earn more."

2. Focus on Abundance, Not Scarcity

A scarcity mindset makes you feel like there's never enough—enough money, time, or resources. This leads to fear and inaction. An abundance mindset, on the other hand, helps you see opportunities everywhere. To cultivate abundance:

- Practice gratitude for what you already have.
- Celebrate small wins and progress.

Financial Mastery for Beauty Professionals:
From $0 to Salon Empire

- Surround yourself with positive, supportive people.

3. Develop a Growth Mindset

A growth mindset is the belief that you can improve through effort and learning. Instead of saying, "I'm not good at managing money," say, "I can learn to manage money better." Focus on continuous improvement, and don't be afraid to make mistakes—they're part of the journey.

4. Set Clear Goals

Wealth starts with a vision. What does financial success look like for you? Write down specific, measurable goals, such as:

- Saving $10,000 in the next year.
- Opening a second salon within three years.
- Investing in a rental property by age 35.

Break these goals into smaller steps and track your progress.

5. Prioritize Long-Term Thinking

A wealth mindset requires delaying gratification. Instead of spending money on short-term pleasures, focus on investments that create long-term value.

Financial Mastery for Beauty Professionals:
From $0 to Salon Empire

Ask yourself: Will this decision bring me closer to or further from my goals?

6. Embrace Accountability

Share your financial goals with a mentor, partner, or trusted friend. Regular check-ins can help you stay on track and motivated.

What You Can Do Right Now

1. Start a Money Journal

Write down your thoughts, feelings, and beliefs about money. Identify patterns that may be holding you back and replace negative thoughts with positive affirmations.

2. Practice Gratitude

List three things you're grateful for every day. This simple habit shifts your focus from what you lack to what you already have.

3. Create a Vision Board

Use images and words to represent your financial goals. Place your vision board somewhere visible to remind yourself of what you're working toward.

4. Take One Small Step

Financial Mastery for Beauty Professionals:
From $0 to Salon Empire

What's one action you can take today to move toward your goals? Whether it's saving $20, researching investment options, or scheduling a meeting with a mentor, start small and build momentum.

Habits to Foster for a Wealth Mindset

1. Daily Affirmations

Repeat affirmations that reinforce your confidence and goals, such as:

- "I am capable of achieving financial success."
- "Every dollar I save is an investment in my future."
- "I am grateful for the opportunities I have to grow."

2. Continuous Learning

Commit to learning something new about personal finance, investments, or business each week. This could be through books, podcasts, or online courses.

3. Surround Yourself with Success

Financial Mastery for Beauty Professionals:
From $0 to Salon Empire

Spend time with people who inspire and motivate you. Join networking groups, attend industry events, or find a mentor.

4. Reflect and Adjust

Regularly review your progress and adjust your strategies as needed. Celebrate your wins, no matter how small, and learn from your mistakes.

Examples of Success: Real-Life Stories

Case Study 1: Jessica's Journey to Abundance

Jessica, a hairstylist, struggled with a scarcity mindset. She often felt like she didn't have enough money, time, or resources to achieve her goals. After attending a financial workshop, Jessica started practicing gratitude and reframed her beliefs about money. She set clear goals, started saving consistently, and invested in advanced training. Today, Jessica owns a thriving salon and mentors other beauty professionals.

Case Study 2: Alex's Growth Mindset

Alex, a nail technician, faced setbacks early in his career, including a failed attempt to open his own salon. Instead of giving up, Alex adopted a growth mindset. He viewed his failure as a learning

Financial Mastery for Beauty Professionals:
From $0 to Salon Empire

opportunity, identified areas for improvement, and tried again. His second salon was a success, and he now owns multiple locations.

Case Study 3: Maria's Accountability Partner

Maria, an esthetician, struggled with emotional spending. She partnered with a colleague who shared similar financial goals. Together, they held each other accountable, shared budgeting tips, and celebrated milestones. Within two years, Maria paid off her debt and saved enough to open her own studio.

Overcoming Emotional Barriers

1. Fear of Failure

Challenge: "What if I try and fail?"
Solution: Reframe failure as feedback. Every setback is an opportunity to learn and grow.

2. Guilt About Earning More

Challenge: "I don't deserve to make more money."
Solution: Remind yourself that financial success allows you to help others, whether it's supporting your family, mentoring others, or giving back to your community.

Financial Mastery for Beauty Professionals:
From $0 to Salon Empire

3. Imposter Syndrome

Challenge: "I'm not good enough to succeed."
Solution: Focus on your skills, experience, and the value you bring to your clients. Remember, confidence grows with action.

The Long-Term Vision: Living with Purpose

A wealth mindset isn't just about making more money—it's about creating a life of purpose, fulfillment, and abundance. It's about using your success to make a difference, whether that's mentoring others, building a legacy, or contributing to causes you care about.

When you break emotional barriers and adopt a wealth mindset, you open the door to unlimited possibilities. You stop reacting to life and start creating it.

Why It's Worth It

Transforming your mindset takes time and effort, but the rewards are immeasurable. A wealth mindset not only improves your financial health but also enhances your confidence, relationships, and overall quality of life.

Financial Mastery for Beauty Professionals:
From $0 to Salon Empire

You have the power to change your story. By shifting your perspective, you can achieve financial freedom and inspire others to do the same.

What's Next?

In the next chapter, we'll explore **Leaving a Legacy: Empowering the Next Generation.** You'll learn how to mentor others, build a business that lasts, and make a lasting impact on your community.

Your mindset is the foundation of your success. Let's continue building the life you deserve.

Chapter 9: Leaving a Legacy: Empowering the Next Generation

What Does It Mean to Leave a Legacy?

Leaving a legacy isn't just about wealth or possessions—it's about the impact you make on others and the values you pass on to future generations. As a beauty professional and business owner, your legacy extends far beyond the services you provide or the money you earn. It's about creating opportunities, inspiring others, and building a foundation that continues to grow and thrive long after you're gone.

Financial Mastery for Beauty Professionals:
From $0 to Salon Empire

In the beauty industry, leaving a legacy means mentoring the next generation of professionals, creating businesses that uplift communities, and using your influence to make a difference. Whether you're teaching someone how to run a successful salon, empowering employees to achieve their goals, or contributing to local causes, your actions can have a ripple effect that lasts for decades.

The Why: The Importance of Leaving a Legacy

1. Create Opportunities for Others

Your success can open doors for others. By mentoring and supporting the next generation, you can help them achieve their dreams while expanding your own impact.

2. Build a Stronger Community

Thriving businesses contribute to thriving communities. By investing in your employees, clients, and local area, you can make a positive difference that extends far beyond your salon.

3. Inspire Future Leaders

Your journey, challenges, and successes can inspire others to pursue their own ambitions. Sharing your

Financial Mastery for Beauty Professionals:
From $0 to Salon Empire

story and knowledge helps build a culture of growth and empowerment.

4. Ensure Longevity for Your Business

By planning for the future, you can create a business that outlasts you. This might mean passing it on to your children, selling it to a trusted colleague, or creating a structure that allows it to operate independently.

The How: Steps to Build and Leave a Legacy

1. Share Your Knowledge

Pass on the lessons you've learned to others. This could include:

- Mentoring employees who aspire to own their own salons.
- Hosting workshops or training sessions for beauty professionals.
- Writing a book or creating online content to share your expertise.

2. Invest in Your Team

Your employees are an extension of your legacy. Support their growth by:

Financial Mastery for Beauty Professionals:
From $0 to Salon Empire

- Offering opportunities for professional development.

- Encouraging them to pursue certifications or advanced training.

- Creating a positive, inclusive work environment where they feel valued.

3. Empower the Next Generation

Consider partnering with local schools, beauty colleges, or community organizations to mentor students or provide internships. This not only strengthens your industry but also builds goodwill in your community.

4. Build a Sustainable Business

A business that relies solely on you isn't sustainable. Create systems and structures that allow your salon to thrive without your constant involvement. This might include:

- Hiring and training managers to oversee daily operations.

- Standardizing processes for client management, marketing, and finances.

- Diversifying income streams to ensure stability.

Financial Mastery for Beauty Professionals:
From $0 to Salon Empire

5. Give Back to the Community

Leaving a legacy isn't just about building a successful business—it's about making a difference. Consider ways to give back, such as:

- Offering free or discounted services to underserved populations.
- Donating a portion of your profits to local charities or causes.
- Sponsoring events or initiatives that benefit your community.

6. Plan for Succession

If you want your business to continue after you step back, you need a clear succession plan. This includes:

- Identifying potential successors, whether they're family members, employees, or external buyers.
- Providing training and guidance to prepare them for leadership.
- Documenting your vision, values, and goals for the business.

Financial Mastery for Beauty Professionals:
From $0 to Salon Empire

What You Can Do Right Now

1. Identify Your Legacy Goals

Ask yourself: What do I want to be remembered for? Write down your goals for creating a legacy, whether it's mentoring others, building a thriving business, or giving back to your community.

2. Start Small

You don't need to make grand gestures to leave a legacy. Begin by mentoring one employee, supporting a local cause, or sharing your knowledge with a colleague.

3. Document Your Knowledge

Create a guide or manual that outlines your business processes, values, and best practices. This ensures your knowledge is preserved and can be passed on to others.

4. Get Involved in Your Community

Look for opportunities to engage with your community, such as attending local events, partnering with schools, or volunteering your services.

Habits to Foster for Legacy Building

Financial Mastery for Beauty Professionals:
From $0 to Salon Empire

1. Teach Regularly

Make it a habit to share your knowledge and skills with others. Whether it's through formal training sessions or informal conversations, teaching helps you solidify your expertise while empowering others.

2. Prioritize People Over Profits

Focus on building strong relationships with your employees, clients, and community. A people-first approach creates loyalty and goodwill that outlasts financial gains.

3. Lead by Example

Your actions speak louder than words. Demonstrate the values you want to pass on—integrity, hard work, and a commitment to excellence.

4. Plan for the Future

Regularly evaluate your business and personal goals to ensure you're working toward a legacy that aligns with your values.

Examples of Success: Real-Life Stories

Case Study 1: Sarah's Mentorship Program

Financial Mastery for Beauty Professionals:
From $0 to Salon Empire

Sarah, a salon owner, created a mentorship program for new beauty professionals. She offered hands-on training, career advice, and financial literacy workshops. Many of Sarah's mentees went on to open their own salons, and Sarah's program became a respected resource in the industry.

Case Study 2: Mike's Community Impact

Mike, a barber, partnered with a local nonprofit to provide free haircuts to homeless individuals. Over time, Mike expanded the initiative to include job training and interview preparation. His barbershop became a hub for community support and empowerment.

Case Study 3: Emma's Family Legacy

Emma built her salon with the goal of passing it on to her children. She involved them in the business from a young age, teaching them the ins and outs of operations, client relations, and leadership. When Emma retired, her children seamlessly took over, continuing her vision and values.

Common Challenges and How to Overcome Them

1. Fear of Letting Go

Financial Mastery for Beauty Professionals:
From $0 to Salon Empire

Challenge: Many business owners struggle with delegating responsibilities or stepping back from daily operations.

Solution: Start small by delegating tasks to trusted employees. Focus on training and building confidence in your team.

2. Lack of Time

Challenge: It's easy to get caught up in the day-to-day demands of running a business.

Solution: Set aside dedicated time each week for legacy-building activities, such as mentoring, planning, or community involvement.

3. Uncertainty About the Future

Challenge: Planning for the future can feel overwhelming, especially in a rapidly changing industry.

Solution: Focus on what you can control, such as creating systems, mentoring others, and building a strong foundation for your business.

The Long-Term Vision: A Legacy That Lasts

Leaving a legacy is about more than what you achieve—it's about the impact you have on others. When you empower the next generation, build a

Financial Mastery for Beauty Professionals:
From $0 to Salon Empire

sustainable business, and give back to your community, you create something that endures.

Your legacy is a reflection of your values, vision, and commitment to making a difference. By focusing on these principles, you can leave the world a better place and inspire others to do the same.

Why It's Worth It

Building a legacy takes time, effort, and intention, but the rewards are immeasurable. It's not just about what you leave behind—it's about the lives you touch and the opportunities you create.

You have the power to shape the future of your industry, your community, and the people around you. By focusing on legacy building, you're creating a ripple effect that will be felt for generations to come.

What's Next?

In the next chapter, we'll explore **Creating a Sustainable Financial Foundation.** You'll learn how to balance personal and business finances, build wealth for the long term, and ensure financial stability for your legacy.

Financial Mastery for Beauty Professionals:
From $0 to Salon Empire

Your legacy starts with the actions you take today. Let's make them count.

Financial Mastery for Beauty Professionals:
From $0 to Salon Empire

Part 4: Financial Mastery and Legacy Building

Chapter 10: Creating a Sustainable Financial Foundation

What is a Sustainable Financial Foundation?

A sustainable financial foundation is the bedrock of lasting success and stability. It's the financial structure that allows you to support your business, invest in growth, and weather challenges without sacrificing your long-term goals. For beauty professionals, this means managing personal and business finances wisely, planning for the future, and ensuring that your money works for you, not the other way around.

Sustainability in finance isn't about earning the most—it's about managing what you have effectively. A well-built financial foundation gives you peace of mind, empowers you to seize opportunities, and enables you to create a legacy that lasts.

The Why: Importance of Financial Sustainability

1. Ensures Stability During Uncertainty

Financial Mastery for Beauty Professionals:
From $0 to Salon Empire

The beauty industry can be unpredictable, with income fluctuations due to seasonality, client turnover, or economic changes. A solid financial foundation provides a safety net during lean times.

2. Enables Strategic Growth

With sustainable finances, you can reinvest in your business, expand services, and explore new opportunities without overextending yourself.

3. Supports Long-Term Wealth Building

A strong financial foundation sets the stage for wealth creation through investments, retirement planning, and business equity.

4. Reduces Stress and Improves Decision-Making

When your finances are in order, you can make decisions with confidence and focus on growing your business, rather than constantly worrying about money.

The How: Steps to Build a Sustainable Financial Foundation

1. Separate Personal and Business Finances

Financial Mastery for Beauty Professionals:
From $0 to Salon Empire

One of the most critical steps in financial sustainability is keeping personal and business finances separate. This ensures accurate tracking, simplifies taxes, and provides a clear picture of your business's performance.

- Open a dedicated business bank account and credit card.
- Pay yourself a consistent salary from your business profits.

2. Create and Stick to a Budget

A budget is your financial roadmap. It helps you allocate resources effectively and avoid overspending.

- **Business Budget:** Include rent, utilities, supplies, marketing, and salaries.
- **Personal Budget:** Cover essentials like housing, groceries, and savings.
- Track your expenses regularly and adjust as needed.

3. Build an Emergency Fund

An emergency fund acts as a financial cushion during unexpected events, such as equipment

Financial Mastery for Beauty Professionals:
From $0 to Salon Empire

breakdowns, slow seasons, or personal emergencies.

- Aim to save three to six months' worth of expenses.
- Start small and contribute consistently.

4. Manage Debt Wisely

Debt can be a useful tool for growth, but it must be managed carefully.

- Avoid high-interest debt, such as credit card balances.
- Use loans strategically for investments that generate returns, like purchasing property or upgrading equipment.

5. Plan for Taxes

Set aside a portion of your income for taxes to avoid surprises during tax season. Work with an accountant to ensure you're taking advantage of all deductions and credits.

6. Diversify Income Streams

Relying on a single source of income can be risky. Diversify your revenue by:

- Selling retail products.

Financial Mastery for Beauty Professionals:
From $0 to Salon Empire

- Offering premium or add-on services.
- Renting booths or spaces in your salon.

7. Invest for the Future

Investments create long-term wealth and financial security. Consider options like:

- Real estate, such as owning your salon's property.
- Retirement accounts, like a SEP IRA or Solo 401(k).
- Stocks, mutual funds, or other investment vehicles.

What You Can Do Right Now

1. Assess Your Current Financial Situation

Take stock of your income, expenses, savings, and debt. Identify areas where you can improve or cut back.

2. Set Financial Goals

Write down short-term, medium-term, and long-term financial goals. For example:

Financial Mastery for Beauty Professionals:
From $0 to Salon Empire

- Short-term: Save $5,000 for an emergency fund within six months.
- Medium-term: Pay off $10,000 in debt within two years.
- Long-term: Buy property for your salon within five years.

3. Start a Savings Plan

Open a dedicated savings account for emergencies or future investments. Set up automatic transfers to make saving a habit.

4. Track Your Spending

Use apps, spreadsheets, or accounting software to monitor your expenses. This helps you identify where your money is going and where you can make adjustments.

Habits to Foster for Financial Sustainability

1. Regular Financial Reviews

Set aside time each month to review your finances. Analyze your income, expenses, and progress toward your goals.

2. Consistent Saving

Financial Mastery for Beauty Professionals: From $0 to Salon Empire

Treat saving as a non-negotiable expense. Even small, regular contributions add up over time.

3. Smart Spending

Before making a purchase, ask yourself: "Is this a need or a want? Does it align with my financial goals?"

4. Ongoing Education

Stay informed about financial management, investments, and industry trends. Read books, attend workshops, or consult with experts.

Examples of Success: Real-Life Stories

Case Study 1: John's Emergency Fund

John, a barber, used to struggle during slow seasons. After attending a financial workshop, he started saving 10% of his income in an emergency fund. Within a year, John had $7,000 saved, which gave him peace of mind and financial stability during a particularly slow winter.

Case Study 2: Sarah's Debt-Free Journey

Sarah, a salon owner, was burdened by credit card debt from starting her business. She created a strict budget, cut unnecessary expenses, and focused on

Financial Mastery for Beauty Professionals:
From $0 to Salon Empire

paying off her highest-interest debts first. In three years, Sarah was debt-free and used her savings to invest in a second salon location.

Case Study 3: Maya's Real Estate Success

Maya, a nail technician, rented her salon space for years but always dreamed of owning her building. She saved consistently, built her credit, and eventually secured a loan to purchase the property. Today, Maya owns the salon and rents out additional space, creating a new income stream.

Overcoming Challenges in Financial Sustainability

1. Inconsistent Income

Challenge: Irregular income makes it difficult to budget and save.
Solution: Base your budget on your lowest-earning months. Save extra income during peak times to cover lean periods.

2. Unexpected Expenses

Challenge: Emergencies can derail your finances.
Solution: Build an emergency fund and maintain insurance coverage for your business and personal needs.

Financial Mastery for Beauty Professionals:
From $0 to Salon Empire

3. Balancing Growth and Stability

Challenge: Investing in growth while maintaining financial stability can be tricky.

Solution: Prioritize investments with high returns and avoid overextending yourself financially.

The Long-Term Vision: Financial Independence

A sustainable financial foundation isn't just about surviving—it's about thriving. By managing your money wisely, you can achieve financial independence, build wealth, and create opportunities for yourself and others.

Financial sustainability also provides freedom. It allows you to focus on what matters most, whether that's growing your business, spending time with loved ones, or pursuing new passions.

Why It's Worth It

Building a sustainable financial foundation takes time and discipline, but the rewards are immense. You'll gain stability, peace of mind, and the ability to pursue your dreams without constant financial stress.

Financial Mastery for Beauty Professionals:
From $0 to Salon Empire

With a strong foundation, you can turn your salon business into a lasting legacy, creating opportunities for future generations and leaving a positive impact on your community.

What's Next?

In the next chapter, we'll explore **Balancing Work and Life as a Beauty Professional.** You'll learn how to avoid burnout, prioritize self-care, and maintain a healthy balance between your professional and personal life.

Your financial future is in your hands. Let's continue building the foundation for your success.

Financial Mastery for Beauty Professionals:
From $0 to Salon Empire

Chapter 11: Balancing Work and Life as a Beauty Professional

Why Work-Life Balance Matters

The beauty industry is fast-paced, demanding, and often requires long hours to build and maintain a thriving business. Many beauty professionals pour themselves into their work, striving to meet client expectations, grow their skills, and build financial stability. While this dedication is admirable, it often comes at the expense of personal well-being.

Work-life balance isn't just about finding time to relax—it's about creating a sustainable lifestyle that supports your physical, mental, and emotional health. When you prioritize balance, you not only improve your quality of life but also enhance your ability to perform at your best, both professionally and personally.

The Why: Benefits of Work-Life Balance

1. Prevents Burnout

Working nonstop can lead to physical and emotional exhaustion, reducing your ability to serve clients and manage your business effectively.

Financial Mastery for Beauty Professionals:
From $0 to Salon Empire

2. Improves Productivity

When you're well-rested and focused, you're more efficient and capable of handling challenges.

3. Enhances Creativity

Downtime allows your mind to recharge, fostering creativity and innovation in your work.

4. Strengthens Relationships

Balancing work with personal time helps you maintain meaningful connections with family, friends, and loved ones.

5. Supports Long-Term Health

Chronic stress from overwork can lead to serious health issues. Prioritizing balance promotes better physical and mental well-being.

The How: Steps to Achieve Work-Life Balance

1. Set Clear Boundaries

Boundaries are essential for maintaining balance. Without them, work can easily bleed into your personal time.

- Establish specific work hours and stick to them.

Financial Mastery for Beauty Professionals:
From $0 to Salon Empire

- Communicate your availability to clients and colleagues.
- Learn to say no to requests that disrupt your balance.

2. Prioritize Self-Care

Taking care of yourself is not a luxury—it's a necessity. Incorporate self-care into your routine, such as:

- Regular exercise to boost energy and reduce stress.
- Healthy eating to support physical and mental health.
- Adequate sleep to recharge and recover.

3. Schedule Downtime

Treat personal time as an important appointment. Block out time for activities that bring you joy, relaxation, or connection, such as:

- Spending time with loved ones.
- Pursuing hobbies or interests outside of work.
- Taking vacations or short breaks to reset.

4. Delegate and Automate

Financial Mastery for Beauty Professionals:
From $0 to Salon Empire

You don't have to do everything yourself. Delegating tasks and automating processes can free up time and reduce stress.

- Hire reliable employees or assistants to handle day-to-day tasks.
- Use technology for scheduling, bookkeeping, and client communication.

5. Practice Mindfulness

Mindfulness helps you stay present and manage stress effectively.

- Start each day with a few minutes of meditation or deep breathing.
- Focus on one task at a time, avoiding multitasking.
- Reflect on what you're grateful for at the end of each day.

6. Evaluate and Adjust Regularly

Work-life balance isn't a one-time achievement—it's an ongoing process. Regularly evaluate your schedule and commitments to ensure they align with your priorities.

Financial Mastery for Beauty Professionals:
From $0 to Salon Empire

What You Can Do Right Now

1. Define Your Priorities

Write down what matters most to you, both personally and professionally. Use these priorities to guide your decisions and schedule.

2. Identify Time-Wasters

Analyze how you spend your time each day. Identify activities that don't align with your goals and eliminate or reduce them.

3. Start Small

Begin with one small change to improve your balance, such as setting a specific end time for work or scheduling a weekly activity you enjoy.

4. Commit to a Self-Care Practice

Choose one self-care activity to incorporate into your routine, like exercising, journaling, or taking a relaxing bath.

Habits to Foster for Work-Life Balance

1. Time Blocking

Financial Mastery for Beauty Professionals:
From $0 to Salon Empire

Dedicate specific blocks of time to work tasks, personal activities, and relaxation. Stick to these blocks to ensure a balanced schedule.

2. Regular Breaks

Take short breaks throughout your workday to rest and recharge. Step away from your workspace to clear your mind.

3. Limit Screen Time

Reduce time spent on social media or other non-essential screen activities. Use that time for meaningful connections or personal growth.

4. Celebrate Wins

Acknowledge your achievements, no matter how small. Celebrating progress helps you stay motivated and maintain a positive mindset.

Examples of Success: Real-Life Stories

Case Study 1: Emma's Boundaries

Emma, a salon owner, struggled with overworking and neglecting her personal life. She implemented clear boundaries, setting work hours and taking Sundays off to spend with her family. Over time,

Financial Mastery for Beauty Professionals:
From $0 to Salon Empire

Emma found herself more focused, productive, and happier in both her work and personal life.

Case Study 2: Carlos' Self-Care Journey

Carlos, a barber, realized his long hours were taking a toll on his health. He started prioritizing self-care by exercising daily and meal-prepping healthy foods. The changes improved his energy levels and made him more effective at work.

Case Study 3: Maya's Delegation Success

Maya, a nail technician turned salon owner, felt overwhelmed managing every aspect of her business. She hired an assistant to handle scheduling and a manager to oversee daily operations. This freed up time for Maya to focus on growth and spend quality time with her children.

Common Challenges and How to Overcome Them

1. Guilt About Taking Time Off

Challenge: Feeling guilty for not working every possible hour.
Solution: Remind yourself that rest makes you more effective and helps you serve your clients better in the long run.

Financial Mastery for Beauty Professionals:
From $0 to Salon Empire

2. Difficulty Saying No

Challenge: Taking on too many commitments out of fear of disappointing others.
Solution: Practice saying no politely but firmly, and prioritize what aligns with your goals.

3. Feeling Overwhelmed

Challenge: Struggling to juggle multiple responsibilities.
Solution: Break tasks into smaller steps, delegate where possible, and focus on one thing at a time.

The Long-Term Vision: A Balanced, Fulfilling Life

Achieving work-life balance isn't just about working less—it's about living more. By prioritizing what truly matters, you can create a life that's both productive and fulfilling.

A balanced lifestyle enables you to sustain your career, nurture relationships, and enjoy the journey. It's not about perfection—it's about making intentional choices that support your well-being and long-term success.

Why It's Worth It

Financial Mastery for Beauty Professionals:
From $0 to Salon Empire

Work-life balance takes effort, but the benefits are profound. It allows you to show up fully for your clients, your loved ones, and yourself. It creates space for joy, creativity, and connection, making life richer and more meaningful.

By finding balance, you're not just building a career—you're building a life you love.

What's Next?

In the final chapter, we'll explore **Your Roadmap to Continuous Growth.** You'll learn how to stay motivated, embrace lifelong learning, and evolve as a beauty professional and entrepreneur.

Your journey toward balance starts today. Let's make it happen.

Financial Mastery for Beauty Professionals: From $0 to Salon Empire

Chapter 12: Your Roadmap to Continuous Growth

Why Growth is a Lifelong Journey

In the beauty industry—and in life—stagnation is the enemy of success. The most successful beauty professionals and entrepreneurs understand that growth isn't a destination; it's a journey. It requires ongoing effort, adaptability, and a willingness to embrace change.

Continuous growth doesn't just apply to your skills or business—it encompasses your mindset, relationships, and personal development. It's about striving to be better today than you were yesterday, no matter how small the improvement.

This chapter provides a roadmap to ensure that your growth never stops, empowering you to reach new heights in your career and personal life.

The Why: Importance of Continuous Growth

1. Stay Ahead in a Competitive Industry

The beauty industry is constantly evolving with new trends, techniques, and technologies. Continuous growth ensures you stay relevant and competitive.

Financial Mastery for Beauty Professionals:
From $0 to Salon Empire

2. Unlock New Opportunities

Growth opens doors. Whether it's expanding your business, attracting high-profile clients, or exploring new revenue streams, personal and professional development creates opportunities.

3. Build Confidence and Resilience

The process of learning and improving builds confidence in your abilities and resilience to overcome challenges.

4. Inspire Others

Your commitment to growth can motivate and inspire your team, clients, and community to pursue their own potential.

The How: Steps to Foster Continuous Growth

1. Commit to Lifelong Learning

The first step to continuous growth is embracing the idea that learning never ends. Stay curious and open to new ideas by:

- Attending workshops, seminars, and conferences.

Financial Mastery for Beauty Professionals:
From $0 to Salon Empire

- Taking online courses to learn new skills or improve existing ones.
- Reading industry publications, books, and blogs to stay informed about trends and best practices.

2. Set and Review Goals Regularly

Growth requires direction. Set short-term, medium-term, and long-term goals for your career and personal life.

- **Short-Term:** Master a new technique or increase client retention by 10% in the next three months.
- **Medium-Term:** Open a second salon or expand your service offerings within two years.
- **Long-Term:** Build a beauty empire or achieve financial independence within a decade.

Review your goals regularly to track progress and make adjustments as needed.

3. Embrace Feedback

Feedback is a powerful tool for growth. Actively seek input from clients, employees, and peers to identify areas for improvement.

Financial Mastery for Beauty Professionals:
From $0 to Salon Empire

- Create a system for collecting client feedback, such as surveys or reviews.
- Conduct regular check-ins with your team to understand their perspectives.
- Be open to constructive criticism and use it as an opportunity to grow.

4. Cultivate a Growth Mindset

A growth mindset is the belief that your abilities and intelligence can improve with effort. To cultivate this mindset:

- Focus on progress, not perfection.
- View challenges as opportunities to learn.
- Celebrate small wins and milestones along the way.

5. Build a Network of Support

Surround yourself with people who inspire and challenge you. Join professional organizations, attend networking events, and seek out mentors who can provide guidance and encouragement.

6. Innovate and Adapt

Growth requires adaptability. Stay ahead of industry trends by experimenting with new techniques, tools,

Financial Mastery for Beauty Professionals:
From $0 to Salon Empire

and technologies. Be willing to pivot when necessary to meet changing client needs or market demands.

What You Can Do Right Now

1. Identify One Area for Improvement

Choose one aspect of your business or personal life to focus on. This could be mastering a new skill, improving client communication, or enhancing your marketing efforts.

2. Create an Action Plan

Write down specific steps to achieve your goal. For example, if you want to improve your social media presence:

- Research best practices for beauty professionals on Instagram.
- Schedule time each week to create and post content.
- Engage with your audience by responding to comments and messages.

3. Seek Out a Mentor

Financial Mastery for Beauty Professionals:
From $0 to Salon Empire

Find someone whose success you admire and ask for their guidance. This could be a salon owner, industry expert, or experienced colleague.

4. Attend an Industry Event

Sign up for an upcoming workshop, trade show, or conference. Use the opportunity to learn, network, and gain fresh inspiration.

Habits to Foster for Continuous Growth

1. Daily Learning

Dedicate time each day to learning something new. This could be watching a tutorial, reading an article, or practicing a technique.

2. Reflection and Self-Assessment

At the end of each day or week, reflect on what you've accomplished and what you can improve. Use this time to celebrate wins and plan your next steps.

3. Goal Setting and Tracking

Make goal-setting a regular practice. Break down your goals into actionable steps and track your progress to stay motivated.

Financial Mastery for Beauty Professionals:
From $0 to Salon Empire

4. Collaboration and Networking

Regularly connect with peers, mentors, and industry leaders to exchange ideas and learn from their experiences.

Examples of Success: Real-Life Stories

Case Study 1: Emily's Skills Mastery

Emily, a hairstylist, committed to learning one new technique each quarter. Over three years, she mastered balayage, extensions, and advanced styling techniques, which allowed her to attract more clients and charge higher prices.

Case Study 2: Carlos' Expansion Journey

Carlos, a barber, set a goal to open a second location within two years. He attended workshops on business management, sought advice from experienced salon owners, and developed a detailed expansion plan. Today, Carlos owns three thriving barbershops.

Case Study 3: Sarah's Social Media Growth

Sarah, a nail technician, struggled to attract new clients. She took an online course on social media marketing and began posting regularly on

Financial Mastery for Beauty Professionals:
From $0 to Salon Empire

Instagram, showcasing her work and engaging with followers. Within six months, Sarah doubled her client base and established a strong online presence.

Overcoming Challenges in Continuous Growth

1. Fear of Failure

Challenge: Worrying that trying something new might not work out.
Solution: Reframe failure as a learning opportunity. Every mistake teaches you something valuable.

2. Resistance to Change

Challenge: Feeling comfortable with the status quo.
Solution: Remind yourself that growth requires stepping out of your comfort zone. Small changes can lead to big results over time.

3. Time Constraints

Challenge: Struggling to find time for personal development.
Solution: Schedule dedicated time for learning and growth, even if it's just 15 minutes a day.

Financial Mastery for Beauty Professionals: From $0 to Salon Empire

The Long-Term Vision: A Life of Purpose and Fulfillment

Continuous growth isn't just about achieving success—it's about creating a life filled with purpose, passion, and fulfillment. By committing to growth, you ensure that your career evolves with you, opening doors to new opportunities and experiences.

Growth also allows you to give back. As you learn and succeed, you can mentor others, contribute to your community, and leave a lasting impact on the industry.

Why It's Worth It

The journey of growth is challenging but deeply rewarding. It pushes you to discover your potential, overcome obstacles, and achieve goals you once thought were impossible.

By embracing growth, you're not just building a successful career—you're creating a life that inspires and uplifts others.

What's Next?

Financial Mastery for Beauty Professionals:
From $0 to Salon Empire

As we conclude this book, it's time to reflect on your journey and take action. You've learned about financial discipline, scaling your business, balancing work and life, and building a legacy. Now, it's up to you to apply these lessons and create the future you envision.

Remember, growth is a lifelong journey. Stay curious, stay motivated, and never stop striving for excellence. Your potential is limitless—embrace it.

Financial Mastery for Beauty Professionals:
From $0 to Salon Empire

Conclusion: The Beauty of Small Steps and Big Visions

As we reach the final page of this journey, it's time to reflect on the transformation we've explored—from a beauty professional perfecting their craft to a business owner building a legacy, and finally, a real estate investor securing long-term wealth.

This book isn't just about strategies and numbers—it's about empowerment. It's about realizing that your journey begins with one small step and that every action, no matter how small, has the potential to create extraordinary change.

Your profession as a beauty expert is the foundation, your business is the bridge, and real estate is the legacy. Together, they form the pillars of a fulfilling, financially stable, and purpose-driven life.

Core Lessons and Rhyme Quotes to Remember

1. Start Small, Dream Big

Big successes come from tiny beginnings. Every dollar saved, every skill learned, and every client served is a stepping stone.

Financial Mastery for Beauty Professionals:
From $0 to Salon Empire

Rhyme Quote:
*"Start with a dollar, a skill, a plan,
Small steps today grow a mighty span."*

---

2. Financial Discipline is Your Compass

Managing your money wisely is the cornerstone of growth. Control emotions, track spending, and reinvest where it counts.

Rhyme Quote:
*"Master your money, don't let it stray,
Discipline now paves a wealth-filled way."*

---

3. Build Your Business Brick by Brick

Owning a business allows you to multiply your income, create opportunities for others, and build a lasting impact.

Rhyme Quote:
*"A business you build with vision and care,
Becomes a ladder to take you anywhere."*

---

4. Real Estate is the Ultimate Investment

Financial Mastery for Beauty Professionals:
From $0 to Salon Empire

Real estate isn't just property—it's a foundation for wealth that grows with time. Use your beauty business to fund and sustain this path.

Rhyme Quote:
"Real estate stands where others may fall,
A wealth that's real, the truest of all."

---

5. Balance is Key to Longevity

Burnout is the enemy of growth. Balance work with self-care, and you'll have the energy to achieve more.

Rhyme Quote:
"Rest and work, in harmony bind,
A balanced life fuels both body and mind."

---

6. Embrace Continuous Growth

Growth doesn't stop when you succeed—it's a lifelong journey. Keep learning, innovating, and challenging yourself.

Rhyme Quote:
"Each day's a step, each goal you meet,
Growth never ends—it's life's heartbeat."

Financial Mastery for Beauty Professionals:
From $0 to Salon Empire

7. Leave a Legacy Worth Celebrating

Your impact is measured not just by what you achieve but by how you inspire and empower others.

Rhyme Quote:
*"A legacy lives in the lives you ignite,
A torch passed on, burning ever bright."*

Take Action: Your Journey Begins Now

You've read the lessons, absorbed the strategies, and reflected on the stories of others who've walked this path. Now it's your turn. Take the first step today, whether it's saving a dollar, setting a goal, or creating a plan.

Small steps lead to big changes. Every decision you make moves you closer to the life you envision—a life of financial freedom, meaningful impact, and unshakable legacy.

Rationale for the Journey

1. **Refined Focus**: This book combines financial discipline with real estate and business ownership, showing you how they work together to create lasting success.

Financial Mastery for Beauty Professionals: From $0 to Salon Empire

2. **Actionable Path**: It provides a roadmap, guiding you from small beginnings to achieving your ultimate goals.

3. **Broader Appeal**: Whether you're a beauty professional, entrepreneur, or aspiring investor, these lessons apply to anyone ready to transform their life.

Closing Thought

Your potential is limitless, and your journey is uniquely yours. The tools are in your hands, the vision in your mind, and the drive in your heart. Believe in the power of small steps, embrace the challenges, and trust that every action brings you closer to your dreams.

Rhyme Quote to Carry Forward:
"One step today, a journey begun,
With each action taken, success is won."

Now, go out and build the life you deserve. The world is waiting for your magic.

Financial Mastery for Beauty Professionals:
From $0 to Salon Empire

The End

Thank You

*"Dreams take root in the smallest seed,
With discipline, they grow and lead.
Build a business, invest with care,
Balance and growth will take you there.
Legacy thrives in the lives you inspire,
Step by step, rise higher and higher."*

— Di Tran
Founder, Di Tran Enterprise

Made in the USA
Columbia, SC
08 February 2025